DRAW KAWAII FANTASY CREATURES

Created by **STEVE HARPSTER**

Leeya

HARPTOONS™ PUBLISHING

Steve Harpster

www.harptoons.com

www.harptoons.com

Harpster, Steve
Draw Kawaii Fantasy Creatures with Number and Letters/ written and illustrated by Steve
Harpster

SUMMARY: Learn how to draw cute fantasy creatures starting with a letter or a number
ART/General, JUVENILE FICTION / General

ISBN 13: 978-0-9995290-3-4
ISBN 10: 0-9995290-3-X

SAN: 859-6921

Follow Harptoons on:

Draw with Steve Harpster at
his website Harptoons.com

For school visit information
www.harptoons.com or
contact Steve Harpster at
steve@harptoons.com

The adventure begins...

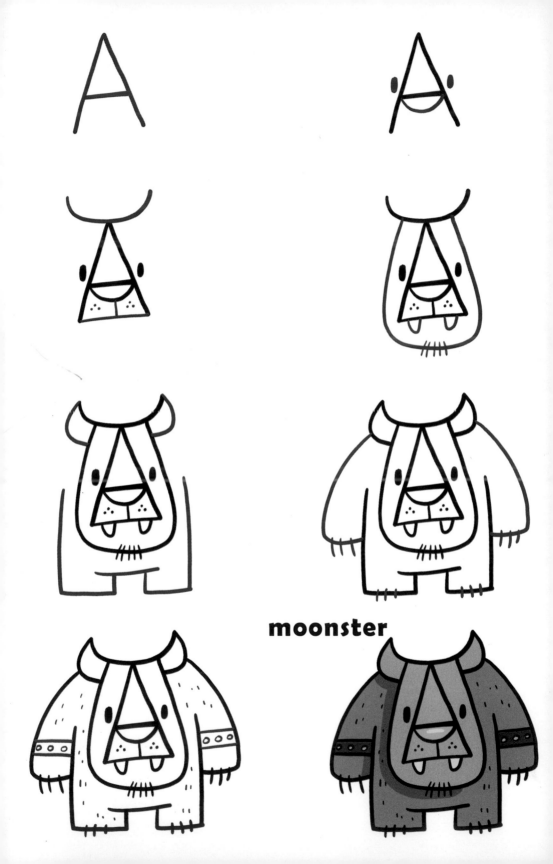

moonster

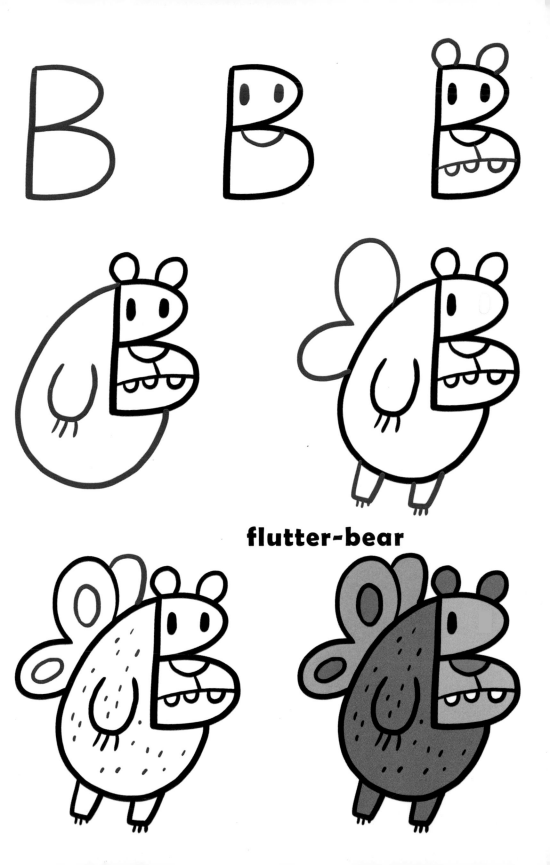

flutter-bear

moonster

griffin

manticore

giant

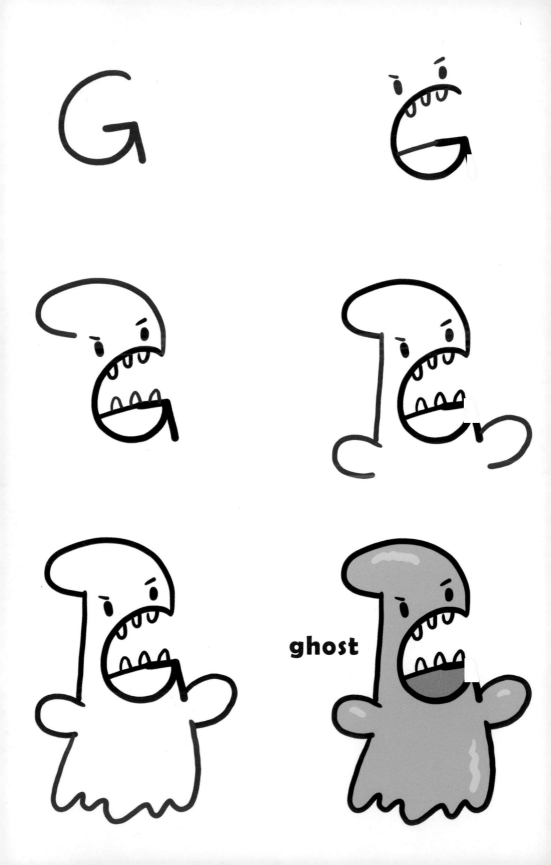

ghost

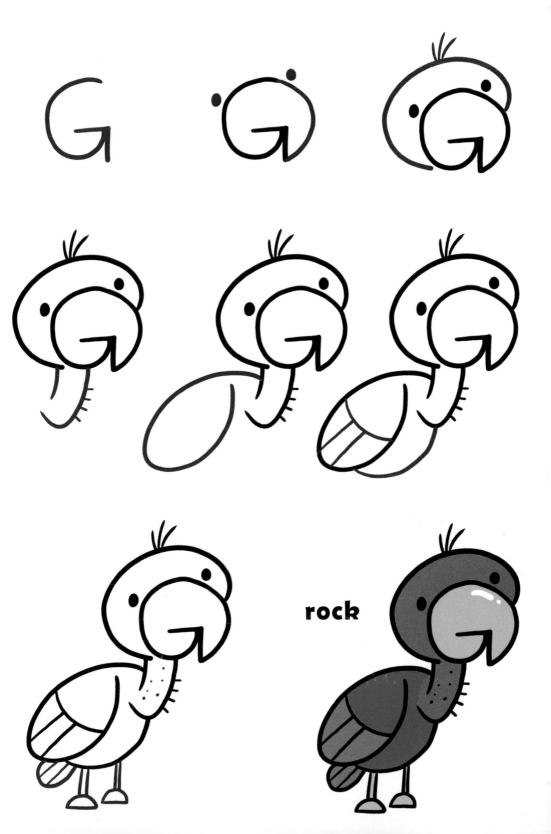

rock

sader

weezard

dragoon

gazellasus

fairy

pegasus

flying fox

water
horse

mermaid

guard
mouse

DANGER

troll

moonster

flying froog

dragoon

gooblin

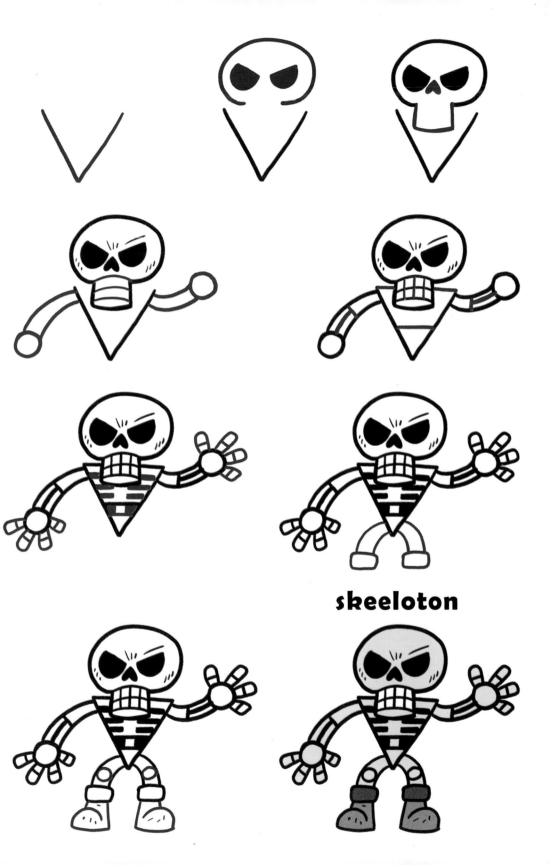

skeeloton

forest eater

Raccoon
Warrior

unicorn

snack

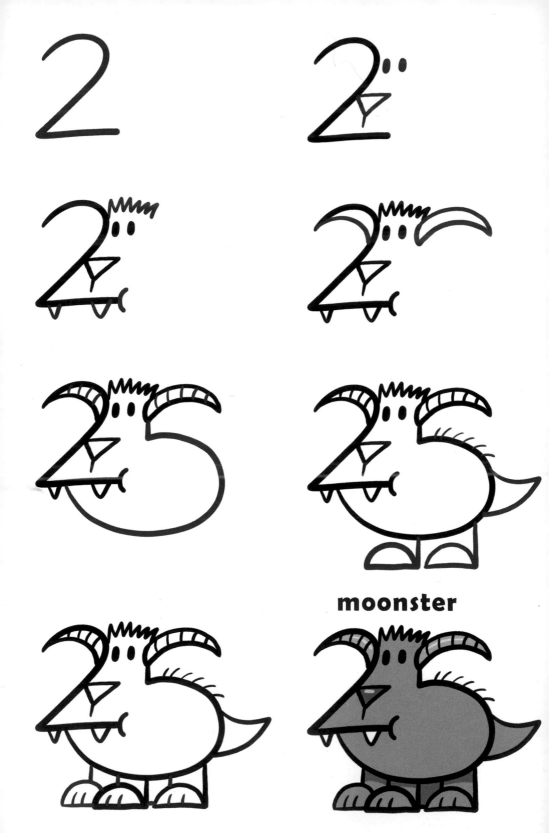

moonster

pega-kita-corn

moonster

weezard-phant

serf

were-wolf

gnome

witch

minotaur

llama-corn

dragoon

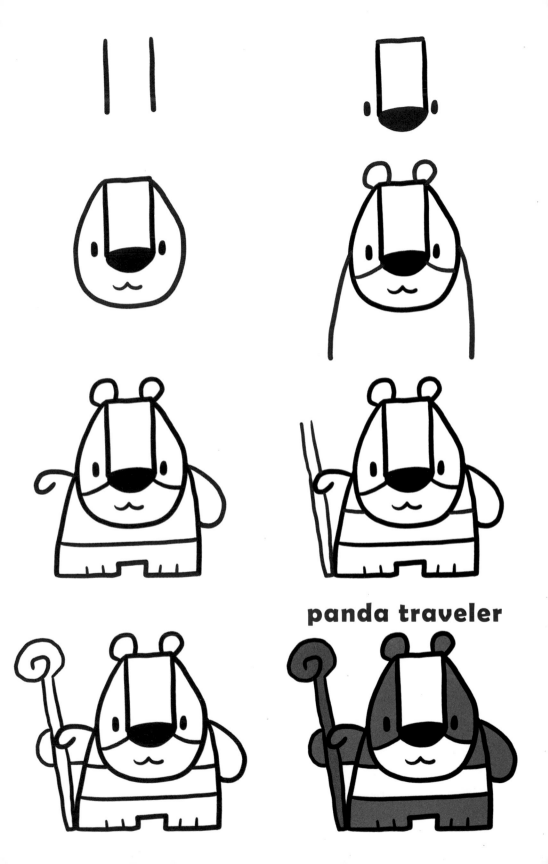

panda traveler

COLLECT EVERY HARPTOONS
HOW-TO-DRAW BOOK AT HARPTOONS.COM

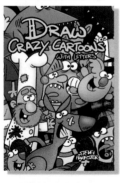

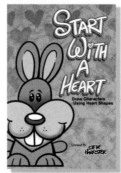